Chronicles of a Sage

Spiritual Revelations via Canto

Deborah Simpson

First Printing

Library of Congress Registration Number: TXu1-356-294

Acknowledgments

A special thank you to fellow authors, Thomas Saint McReynolds, Mark Cotterman, Donna Webster, and Author/Poet Lorinne Pippen for your undying support and encouragement.

ISBN # 978-0-6151-8897-3

<u>Dedication</u>

I dedicate the *Chronicles of a Sage* series to my son, Nicholas. I am proud of you for whom you are, for your determination, for your relentless spirit, for your heart of gold and for holding steadfast to your convictions. I am honored to call you my son.

-- I love you, Mom

Table of Contents

Introduction 11

Chapter 1 – The Rising
Advantage 14
Contented 15
Peace 16
My Beloved 17
False Filament 19
In Mute, So Wise 20
Give To Me 21
A Rendering of Wisdom 22

Chapter 2 – Meditation
Inside Out 26
Torn 28
Fraught 29
For Now, For Always 31
Tomorrow, Today 32
Passion 33
Providence 35
Decision 37
Unbridled 39
Discarded 40
Thinking of You 41
A Rendering of Spirit 43

Chapter 3 – Introspection
Saddled 46
Ordained Clamor 47
Season's Reach 48
And, Still 49
Chastity 50
This Love 51
Immersed 52
Chantilly 53
Coax Her Out 54
Surrender 55
I Am 57
A Rendering of Exploration 59

Chapter 4 – Encounter
Stale Mate 62
Underrated 63
The Storm 64
My Knight, Tonight 65
And He, And He 66
Withered 67
Callous 68
Forgotten 70
Simply A Virtue 72
Never Gone 73
And Yet 74
A Rendering of Self 76

Chapter 5 – Deliberation
Voodoo 80
Ethereal Circlet 81
My Knight: A Classic Ode 82
River Dance 83
Wedded 84
Would You 85
Just Another Day 87
Vaguely Precise 88
Quietly Numbed 89
Vividly Blind 90
Lover 91
Unforgettable 92
A Rendering of Stature 93

Chapter 6 – The Quest
Rest Sweet, The Flail 96
Beautiful 97
Reflection 99
Dimly Bright 100
Ageless Age 101
Though 102
Scarred 103
In Waking Sleep 104
Hopeless 105
Sense Beyond Sense 106
Ousted 107
A Rendering of Existence 108

Chapter 7 – Fall to Rise
Reverberating Lone 112
Left 113
Hollow 114
Your Mistake 115
Tundra 116
True 117
Negated 118
Renovate Me 119
Faith in Purpose 121
Hands of Avarice 122
Eddy 123
Pieces of You 124
A Rendering of Pain 126

Chapter 8 – Energy
Gifting Elements 130
The Rose 131
Doppelganger 133
The Audacity 135
Egyptian Throng 136
Embellished Grapple 137
This Kiss 138
Sanctify Me 140
A Rendering of Know 141

Chapter 9 – Detonation
Inheritance 144
Immortal Love 146
Purged 147
Unwanted 148
Lay Down, My Arms 150
Resoluteness 151

Luminosity 152
Consecration 153
As One 154
Reckon 155
Interpretation 156
Stripped 158
Fare Not, To Fare 159
Shaman's Prayer 160
A Rendering of Beyond 162

Chapter 10 – Soar
The Artisan's Blade 166
Gallantry 167
A Rejoinder 168
Cyprian 169
Abandoned 170
Kismet 171
Fallen 172
Incarnation 174
Unguarded 175
Taut the Night 176
Resounding Blind 177
Repetitive Epoch 178
The Phoenix of Raven 179
Emancipation 180
A Conduit for Dawn 181
Heaven's Deliverance 182
Peripheral Edge 183
Uncloaked 184
Contenting Breeze 185
Begging Not to Wither 186
A Solitary Embrace 187
Tears 188
Annihilation 189

A Final Rendering 190
Inspirational Quotes 191

Introduction

The human spirit is an infinite bounty and much like the air, is not subject to interpretation. Its wisdom often remains undefined as its abundance is often incommunicable. There are times we do not understand our own strength, we just know it is there. At times we do not understand our capacity to love, it just is. We are able to forgive the transgressions against us and have no idea why that is.

Have you ever felt stifled within the confines of your daily routine? Have you ever found yourself asking the question, "Why me?" Has there ever been a time in your life when you ask, "What about me?" Have you ever felt like life has pinned you up against the wall and you have no way of getting off of it? Are there times in your life when you feel emotionally detached? Did you ever ask yourself, "What am I doing with my life?" Has the question, "Where am I going in life" ever crossed your mind? Have you ever looked around you to realize that your life is nothing like you envisioned it to be? Do you ever have feelings of doubt, hopelessness or restlessness? Do you ever feel like just giving up? If any of this sounds familiar or if you feel you can add to these questions, you are not alone.

The following chapters of free-verse are untamed, being categorized in the exact order they were written. I invite you to journey with me along a poetic tale of philosophical ponderings, spiritual musing, consideration of pain, envisages of love and visualizations of the supernatural. Concluding each chapter of verse, you will delve into the revelations inspired by the deliberation of the written word.

Welcome, one and all.

Chapter 1 - The Rising

Advantage

It Is Wisdom,

So Fashionably Cloaked

By the Appearance of Youth –

That Conquers,

Treachery Trudged –

At Any Age.

<u>Contented</u>

Stepping out of the bath,
That solitary morn-
Naked, dripping wet,
To my knees, I fell.

The blood, my spirit,
Poured like rain, my eyes-
Desolate shock moved my lips,
Mercy begged for heal.

Into ashes I crumbled,
Energy drained into vacuity-
Feebly, arose to stand,
Floated into night.

Peace engulfed, somehow,
Igniting strength, inspiration-
Spirit's blood ran dry,
Pain ran insipid, my heart.

Welkin love embraced,
Introducing me to I-
God's beautiful child,
I, He has carried.

Peace

If you were here before me,
Right now-
My arms would completely
Enwrap you.

My head would gently sigh,
Atop your chest-
While listening to
The comforting rhythm-
Of your knowing heart.

I would breathe in your beauty,
That perfect peace-
Flowing from you,
Through me.

My Beloved

My spirit sleeps,
Calm the wind –
Eclipsing my mind,
With reverie;

Hint of you,
In mystic whisper –
My heart quivers,
Slow the night –

My body rests,
Alone with you –
Your aura caressing,
My skin;

Enchanted air,
Warms my nudity –
Alluringly mounting,
My desire –

My dreams sigh,
Secure the night –
Your essence blankets,
My fear;

My passion,
Breathing through you –
Bliss, is the silence,
You so pervade –

My wings soar,
Comforted the sun –
Mine eyes,
They weep repose;

Vision, no longer,
Be it deflected –
My contentment resides,
Within you.

False Filament

Your mime –
Pales adjacent,
To the clouds
Of jasper –

Intrepidly dallying –
In spade,
Around your
Sanctimoniousness –

It is your –
Ostentatious Adoption,
Predicating your
Vacillation –

While hallmarking –
Your presence,
Falsely within
Credulous mind –

Your acquisition, -
Only a veneer,
So eyes remain
Stale of sight –

Alighted in realm –
Of falsity,
The air
You so ignite.

In Mute, So Wise

It is your heart that drips –
Ache within the silence your mind –
As night finds your body restless –
Aside the woman you have chosen –

It is your pride that distresses –
Need within the chambers your soul –
As day illuminates your love –
Afar from the woman you crave –

It is your abandon that urges –
Return to the beauty your memory –
It is guilt punishing your reconcile –
This decision you so have made –

It is your want that pleads –
Rectifying of your feral choice –
Your dispassion fuels now your touch –
As heart remains dedicated to yearn –

It is your tomorrow that hints –
Removal of arrogance your elation –
Your fear thwarts rigid your intuition –
As soul continues beg for release.

Give To Me

My child so weak
Take my air
So you may breathe

My baby in pain
Give to me your hurt
So I may suffer

Take from me
My body, my spirit
That you may be free

Will to me your suffer
My most precious
I love you, my son

A Rendering of Wisdom

Age merely begets years. Wisdom defies the laws of age. For those who do not seek, no matter what the age, shall never attain. Wisdom is not an avail to the elderly. It is an honor bequeathed to one's soul at birth. It is only those attuned to said honor that will attain its virtue enough to share of its wealth.

While it certainly is the accumulation of life's events that makes one knowledgeable, it is the spirit and the energy of youth that continues into the brilliance of wisdom. It is the youth's vigor that teaches the aged. Quite often, as we progress in age, we allow ourselves to lose the essential requisites of life. We discard our innocence. We abandon hope. We disown our purity to love and replace it with fear from anguish. And yet, when we are given to come face to face with the absolute limpidness of a merry child, we dismiss it with what we deem to know. We call a child naïve. We say the child will learn eventually, so let the enjoyment last as long as it may.

What we fail to realize, however, is that we have personally failed ourselves by allowing heartache to saturate our core. By permitting the depravity of numbness to engorge your heart and mind, your ability to grow and learn ceases. When you dismiss the openness of youth, the consequence you instill within yourself is the rejection of your very own progression. Hence, no matter how old you are, your attainment is, therefore, stymied.

The elderly believe acumen to be the fruit of their life's labor, when in fact, this belief slights their honor. It is when we become open to youthful voices, that the virtue of wisdom is rekindled. Children are and continue to be our source of enlightenment as it is their inexperience that fosters our continuous growth. Keep your heart and your mind open, as wisdom truly is attained through those who remain naïve in heart, despite what life has taught.

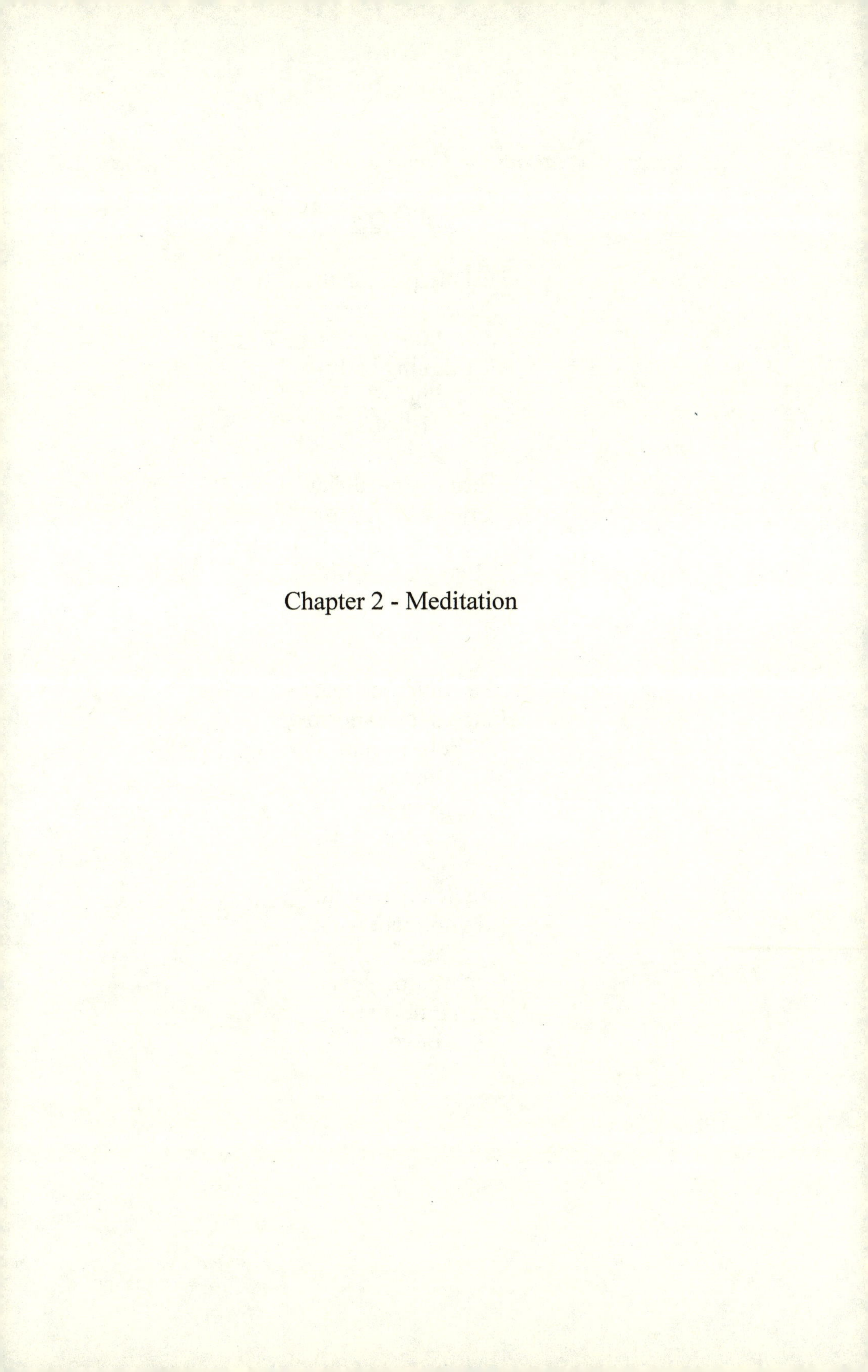

Chapter 2 - Meditation

Inside Out

Feel my passion that
Begs your entry
Into my
Yearning body
Sighing
Bliss

Hear my need that
Cries with release
With your
Every unselfish
Gentle
Thrust

See my mind that
Hungers for tomorrow
Your insight
Into my
Burning
Heart

Cradle my soul that
Lies dormant within
My flesh
Awaiting your
Embrace
Beyond

Seize our union that
Hovers lusty air
Musing over
Our intuitive
Expressive
Tongue

Caress my eyes with
Your mystical know
While culminating
Our heaven
Rhythmical
Serene

Torn

Shrouded through empathy
Lies unadorned whispers
Of apologies for mistakes
Made against the grieving

Realizations are made
Timing not always ideal
When heart undrapes itself
Despite its musty veil

Tears return dry to bleed
Resuming their yearn
Yet plans, they've been made
Sorrow so sweetly replies

Internal struggle surges
Dividing spirit from reality
It is the choice of soul
That brings tears of joy

Fraught

There are times when
Strength withers
From this, my spirit
That so enriches you

There are moments when
Hope drains
From this, my heart
That so inspires you

There are nights when
Dreams vanish
From this, my vision
That so enlivens you

There are days when
Light hides from
Within these, my eyes
That so beautify you

There are moments when
Smile vanishes
From this, my mouth
That so joys you

There are times when
Life weights
Atop these, my shoulders
That so comfort you

This is the season when
Autonomy begs
For arms of compassion
As mine are numb

For Now, For Always

For Now

I am your partner in your aloneness –

I am your strength when yours has vanished –

I am your sanity when yours has strayed –

I am your light when darkness has covered your eyes –

For always.

Tomorrow, Today

Dreams are the whispers
Of destiny's embrace,
Wherein introspective muse
Prospers its purpose –

Thoughts are our nuisance
Intercepting our soar,
Within which so analytical
Denying our spirit –

Contentment is the vision
Reigning our fear,
That continues to thrive
Complementing our need –

Today is the antidote
For hesitancy's plague,
That chimes its bells
For only listen.

Passion

Contemplate me
Over
Morning
Coffee

Ponder me
During
Evening
Wine

Reflect me
Within
Daytime
Lull

Sense me
Along
Leisurely
Drive

Touch me
With
Your
Mind

Experience me
Through
Your
Heart

Erect me
Within
Your
Spirit

Envision me
Completing
Your
Need

Ponder your
Contemplation
Of
I

Providence

You retract
While reaching –
For
Bolshie
Stubbornness –

You hide
Within light –
While
Grasping,
For cover –

You scream
Silent Covet –
Through
Deadpan
Words –

You admit
While searching –
For
Justifiable
Denial –

You Feel,
Beyond yourself –
And
Beg
Release –

You continue
To fathom –
While
Daring
Escape –

Fate draws
Closer, despite –
Your
Futile
Grapple –

Decision

The droplets of time,
Seize the tow
Of yesterday's
Current –

The drape of sun,
Ignites reluctance
Of Today's
Enigma –

The sands of moon,
Endow awareness
To core's
Requisite –

The light of spirit,
Relentlessly ignites
Ashen flame's
Fire –

The flight of mind,
Inevitably chokes
Heart's true
Desire –

The filaments of desire,
Eternally intensify
Vision's piercing
Need –

The chamber of avowal,
Seizes the tow
Of Today's
Indecision.

Unbridled

I reflected your awe today,
So the rhythm of your heart
Would beat tranquil –
In love.

I cried into the sky today,
So the rain of my tears
Would drench you –
In faith.

I smiled into the sun today,
So the ray of my light
Would saturate you –
In joy.

I caressed the river today,
So the ripples of my tide
Would embrace you –
In kind.

I sighed into the moon tonight,
So the dreams of your night
Would soar infinitely –
In heaven.

Discarded

Did you ever feel
Abandoned,
By your heart that
Loves

While ignoring the
Silence,
Of the reasons it
Shouldn't –

Did you ever feel
Lost,
By your mind that
Wanders

To the embrace of
Love,
Even if it for only
Once –

Did you ever feel
Yearn,
Within the speak of
Another

Whose words epitomize your
Dream,
Through the trail of their
Dust –

Thinking of You

Thoughts of you never cease
To permeate my mind
I find myself anxiously
Awaiting you

This feeling is nothing
Less than love and
Desperately yearns
To grow

But this love is at halt
Meandering in dryness
As you are
Its water

The water that hides
From me, but the water
Nonetheless so igniting
My thirst

I beg you not a mute
And do so request your
Speak to me, in love
Or otherwise

I bid my ask that you
Breathe your words as
A whisper into
My ear

I ask of your touch,
Your embrace, your arms
To enwrap me with
Tender security

That I may give unto
You that which I have
Never so dared
To give

The give of my passionate
Heart that breathes you
Every day and prays that
You fight

To unlock your heart
And relinquish its beauty
To me, so it may beat
With mine

I am lonely without you
And continuing is the
Silence of my love, dripping
In isolation

A Rendering of Spirit

Often times we get caught up in our daily routines which causes doubt, apprehension and anxiety about what tomorrow may bring. We tend to concentrate too heavily on the tangibles facing us, that we evade our ethereal existence. By setting aside the most important deliberations of spirit, inevitably we become consumed with fear, restlessness and negativity. Our physical existence in the world cannot be denied and is very important. However, attending to our physical existence without giving equal attention to our chi is detrimental.

Step back for a moment and examine what it is that is going on in your life now or what has occurred that keeps you from exuding the positive energy that is you. Brooding negativity is as a result of physical and/or emotional circumstances that you allow to manifest. Whether you do this consciously or subconsciously are of no relevance. What is significant is that you deliberately make the persistent effort to draw upon the central hub of every obstacle and extract from it only the importance of its teaching. The useless remains, i.e. the exacting factor, need to be discarded immediately. Once you thrust aside exacting factors, you allow the emanation of spirit.

Your essence is your true source of mettle and tranquility. Too often, we tend to snub our inner fulfillment by concentrating too heavily on our physical needs. It is then that we become imbalanced. God's creation of the human spirit is abundant and flawless. Likewise, your physical design is also faultless. It is when you place the monumental fixation upon your physical attributes without divvying equal attention to your core that creates a disproportion between the two. This is extremely injurious to both you and all of those around you. Your concentration must be centered on the inner you. Meditating on the voice of spirit will unite soul with mind renewing God's perfection.

If you feel stifled or confused, look to yourself for the answers. It is likely you are the one holding yourself down by ignoring the substance of truth your spirit continuously tries to unveil to you. Acceptance of your immortal self will foster the rebirth of who you truly are and will put asunder the insecurities that have caused your anxieties and doubt. You will begin to find strength where you thought was none. You will begin to re-examine your forgotten dreams that you thought were impossible to attain. Once you allow your hope to be restored, you give your faith the power to trounce negativity and tackle the obstacles that face you with renewed passion.

Absoluteness is attained when looking through eyes of vision.

Chapter 3 - Introspection

Saddled

I ran to the gully to where
My stallion used to ride me –
At that flecked furrow we'd dream,
Before trotting to river's edge -

I hurried to the gully in search
Of that worn saddle I'd mount –
Riding atop gallantry's heir,
Replacing my need with dignity -

A momentary sit, I stared in fondness
At the gentle imprint of his hoof –
Freedom's master he surely was,
Graceful with pride, indubitably -

I walked to the river to where
Tranquility taught us rest –
Quiet hush draped with current,
As we'd drink nature's wine –

I strolled to the pebble bed in search
Of that soft saddle I'd grip –
When my spirit journeyed strained,
Upon my steed's back; its noble home -

I ran back to the gully to look
Behind the ravine's moss gate –
I cried one silken tear,
Moistening a broken saddle.

Ordained Clamor

The corners of my eyes spit ice chips
Through their blazing vision –
Inaudible, my tongue through glued lips
Enticing the vociferous silence –

The air in my breath rained cotton
Through its dampened speak –
Careless, my limbs to numbing touch
Consequentially oblivious to resolution –

The fall of my step slid uncontested
Even through its reconciled stance –
Foreboding clarity's indistinctness
Inaugurating ingenious retrospection –

It was solely the eve of my kismet
That ran blind to that open door –
Eschewing mortality's advantage
Over such - my innocent heart

Season's Reach

It was the
Stillness of the wind,
Cascading breeze
Through night -

That whispered
Tomorrow's dream,
Within today's
Reflection -

It was the
Clarity of the sun,
Shining faintly
Upon day –

That smiled
Through clouds,
Gently serenading
Anxiety –

It was the
Melody of the air,
Enlivening hope
Within chaos –

That flowered
Yesterday's innocence,
Steadying flight
Of Today

And, Still

My breath,
Listlessly breathes –
My eyes,
Torpidly see -

My flesh,
Abysmally rumples –
My ears,
Scarcely hear –

My legs,
Maladroitly move –
My hair,
Sparsely falls –

My fingers,
Intransigently decline –
My speak,
Surely diluted -

And, still,
You say –
You love,
Me.

Chastity

Faded glory shone down
On me this morn,
Like trailing light
From a once adored sun –

Hidden tears showered upon
Me this ponderous eve,
Like overcast air
Hovering a forgotten lake –

Eccentric notions swayed firm
Through my mind aimlessly,
Like drifting feathers
Freed from their dove –

Flighty dreams abruptly halted
Their mystical weave today,
Like molten hailstones
Falling in stark contradiction –

Intrinsic love yelled quietly
Through lips glued shut,
Like youth's forethought
Into yesteryear's desertion

This Love

You breathe life into
This, my dormant heart –
You calm the restlessness
These years have offered –

You accompany my mind with
Brilliant understanding –
You captivate my spirit
With twinned desire –

Your spoken creed croons
Rejuvenation into my faith -
Your unspoken valor permits
My descent into love –

Your reticent élan discovers
All that I've fussily buried –
Your gentleness so invites
My emancipation into you -

Your hand in mine relieves
This heart's restive journey –
I pray this peace persevere,
With you, I am at one.

Immersed

Your lips breathe my thoughts
Without my utterance –
As my heart bleeds you
In love without your touch –

Your arms embrace my need
Without my ask –
As my tears cry you
In loneliness without –

Your eyes see my soul
Through my flesh –
Resting my dreams within
The comfort of you –

Your vigor exceeds my logic
Captivating my sight –
Reawakening my spirit into
Love with you

Chantilly

Plagiarize my words within
Your mind, that they
May speak themselves
Into your spirit –

Memorialize my wrath within
Your equanimity, that it
May captivate your
Internal composure –

Serialize my jauntier within
Your gentile, that it
May accompany your
Welkin faith –

Anesthetize my irrational within
Your creed, that it
May never hinder
Your nurtured squire -

Bastardize my squander within
Your resolve, that it
May never infiltrate
Your immortal beauty –

Fantasize my flightiness within
Your choice, that it
May keep grounded
Your answered desires

Coax Her Out

She's walked alone for
All these years;
Pen to paper flowed
Her laden heart –

Her tears dripped solo
Into pool of isolation;
Resistance lost to
Creation of callous wall –

Yet inside, bruised heart
So helplessly beats;
A frightened little girl
Behind a woman's shield –

She begs for security
In silence, though;
She searches for release
Within his love –

She cries for understanding
In quiet, though;
She thirsts for strength
When her stubborn yells –

She's walked alone for
All these years;
Pen to paper flows
In hope his hear

Surrender

I found you staring into
Distance, these recent days –
Feeling the drift, your
Intensity floating away –

The air in my breath returns
With your loving speak –
But fails me, it does
When distress embraces you –

I ask your lean upon me
In your times of need –
My heart trembles in beg
Of your surrender to I -

When your world crumbles
I am for your elixir -
When pressure bears its weight
I shall provide your rest –

When the wall draws your back
I am for your tender removal –
When your mind verges explosion –
I shall provide your retreat –

When seclusion finds you lonely
I am your companion in lone -
When your spirit feels dejected –
I shall provide your serenity –

When your kindness is unappreciated
I am for your reminder –
When your heart goes hungry –
I shall replenish you

I Am

The pillow that catches
Your tears -
The tissue that pats
Your eyes -

The blanket that warms
Your nakedness –
The couch that cradles
Your body –

The comforting creases in
Your pants –
The feel of soft cotton in
Your shirt -

The smell of sweetness in
Your food –
The taste of relief in
Your beer -

The sun that greets
Your morning –
The breeze that caresses
Your hair –

The rain that cleanses
Your flesh –
The towel that dries
Your beauty –

The heart that beats for
Your love –
The smile that refuses
Your frown –

The air that replenishes
Your breath –
The one that accompanies
Your silence

A Rendering of Exploration

Exploration of self provides an abundance of knowledge. By opening your eyes and looking inside of yourself, you will bring to light your fears, your doubts, and worries. You also, however, discover your strengths, your ambitions, your wants, and needs. Growth of self is cultivated through the recognition of spirit. By feeding your strengths to overcome your weaknesses, you allow for the abolishment of pain and destituteness of heart.

When you take the time to acquaint yourself with you, you become an adept reader of your intuition. When nurtured, presentiments will provide for you an endless source of encouragement, support and guidance. Equally, remaining aloof to the guide of your instincts, you become saturated with confusion. Ignorance of your internal decree bequeaths a lack of good judgment. Did you ever say to yourself, "I shouldn't have done that?" Have you ever found yourself thinking, "I should have listened to myself?"

Simply put, intuition is the golden thread that binds the conscious with the spirit. If your intuition steers you forward, go forward. Did you ever wish you could go back in time to do something you didn't do? Have you ever done something and wished you had not?

Did you ever meet someone and wish you could figure them out? To learn of others, you first have to discover yourself. Do you ever find yourself questioning why it is you seem to attract the wrong types of people to you? Oppositely, have you ever encountered the right type of person, yet you seemed to be repelled by them? The answer is because you have not taken the time to realize who it is you are. By not spending time on essential self-exploration, you allow for insecurity of self to govern. Ultimately, this will leave you feeling like you are "not good enough" or that you are "undeserving" of love, peace, fulfillment or contentment.

Exploration of self is the essential key to knowledge, freedom of insecurity, and the road to self-harmony.

Chapter 4 - Encounter

Stale Mate

And the clock, so it chimes
Its final bell within the night –
Silently it booms within the bines
Where rests the elite, out of sight -

Morning comes without the know
Still striding in yesterday's tick –
Afternoon dampens with vacant show
As this night now flickers, so sick –

And the call of a shadowed voice
Culminates the crimson prattle –
Jaundice, his irrational choice
To leave her abandoned to rattle –

And the clock, so it sleeps
Deafeningly piercing the air –
The elite opposes her weeps
As the wine is hers to bear –

Underrated

And so the final toast bids,
Although, only to I you fool –
For my shimmering veil of beauty
That remains, despite your humbug –

Your deception shall not abrade
My tender heart, as you undeserving –
It be only for your nefarious soul,
That your heart beats bloodless –

If not for your incoherent tongue
Speaking disjointedly your mind,
Hindsight would provide for comfort –
Not for volatile, internal unrest –

Time shall issue your justification,
But will never offer its commiseration –
Lethargic strife will only inure,
As secular choice spawns poverty –

Memories only bear witness to truth;
Your spirit beleaguers when not regarded –
My oath I shall abide; never to bother,
Your spirit continues my speak to you -

The Storm

It flummoxes the wind so flailing,
To the west grazing the crops -
While spurious rain pours lifeless,
Out of its shuttering wings –

It streams the air with silence,
Thunder its sinister laugh –
Festooned with caricatured lightening
Breathing its unsettling chill –

It cries the night alone in the east,
Jousting filaments of sand –
Burying the hologram of love,
Within prophetic contradiction -

It adjudicates the tranquility,
Reigning paramount in the south –
Jesting the sky with tornado,
Its need for total supremacy –

It bends the air in the north,
Bending fearless, the hearts of man –
Showering its brooding obduracy,
Within the hearts of the unsuspecting –

My Knight, Tonight

I challenged your offers today,
Even those of your gifting hands –
With stubbornness and indifference
That you overcame with strength –

I tempted your criticism tonight,
Only to be met with accolade –
Even through my glossy rationale
Your assured caress upon my cheek –

I memorialized our forgotten years,
As our sighs gently kissed –
The smile you brought to my son
Never before silenced, so my voice -

I fell asleep in your eyes tonight,
As the whisper of pureness fell down –
And the echo of peace so surely
Embraced my shattered dreams –

And He, And He

It was all about the look
I had on that particular day,
That he decided I to be his prey –
And then he moved on –

It was all about the intrigue
I dazzled his mind that day,
That he decided I to be his game –
And then he moved on –

It was all about the disinterest
I showed him during that time,
That he decided I his target –
And then he moved on –

It was all about the independence
I exuded throughout his quest,
That he felt compelled to nail –
And then he moved on -

It was all about the chase
That grabbed him and made him play,
That he felt distinguished to toss me –
And then, he moved on –

Withered

Wilts the rose through a violet thorn
Under twilight of intrepid dawn –
Sewn are the strings of tide
Chaotically strewn are their tracks –

A misfit shielded within acquiescence
Yet blaringly naked, nonetheless –
Eyes bejeweled with lustrous pride
Hiding the indecency of shame –

The unwanted truth so bears its fruit
Within the labors of age –
As fatigue finds its home, these bones
Dreams placed rightfully, in sleep –

Stands violet thorn through wilting rose
Under dawn of intrepid twilight –
The strings of tide so adroitly sewn
Their tracks strewn in chaos –

Callous

Your voice
Sighed
My
Tremble

My heart
Pounded
Your
Indifference

Your jest
Insulted
My
Know

My care
Wilted
Your
Spirit

Your stare
Exposed
My
Future

My futile
Attempt
Fell
Grave

Your mimic
Mocked
My
Love

My final
Words
No
Matter

Forgotten

The sun
Yet
She
Rises

Even though
Beg
Hollers
Not

Eyes yen
For
Night's
Recluse

The stars
Shine
Even
Still

Though not
In
This
Sky

Only dimly
Glimmer
They
Do

For this
Sky
Shines
Not

Under which
Dreams
Not
Worthy

Why still
The
Sun
Rise

Simply A Virtue

My prophecy, a legend -
Some would say beyond
The darkness of doubt,
As I speak its nectar –

Eccentric my expression -
So some have said
While maladroitly rapt,
Within intensity's acumen –

My prospect, desired –
So I've been told
By those with faint voice,
Gazing in admiration –

My wrapping, a conquest –
So I've been shown
Through the eyes of those,
Ashamed of whom they are –

My essence, a mystery –
So still remains
As seen through eyes,
Masked by sight –

Never Gone

If your heart should cry,
I shall come to you, my dear
And with gentle breath –
Lovingly dry your tears –

If you should ever need,
I shall be by your side
And with comforting breeze –
Surround you in ease –

If your soul should grieve,
I shall stay with you, my love
And enwrap you with wings -
Until your flight secured –

If you should ever despair,
All you need do is whisper
And I shall hold you until –
You advise me to rest –

If you are ever lonely,
Remember I am always with you
Simply close your eyes –
And dream me alive –

And Yet

I've learned to dance
When I just want to sleep;
I've learned to laugh
When I just want to cry;

I've learned to walk
When I can't even stand;
I've learned to sing
When I can't even talk;

I've learned to love
Those who've wronged me;
I've learned to forgive
Those who don't even ask;

I've learned to give
Even to those who take;
I've learned to accept
Even that which I fear;

I've learned to give up
Pride for the sake of another;
I've learned to forsake
Need for the want of another;

I've learned to never ask
For what I truly desire;
I've learned to never speak
About what I truly dream of;

I've learned to live life
For the good of others;
And yet I have still to learn
To live life for my own good

A Rendering of Self

We often find ourselves stifled within the conformity of our daily routine. There are days when you just don't feel like getting out of bed. Every day seems like it starts out the same and pretty much continues with no change until evening. Of course, there is the occasional something that comes along providing for a bit of excitement, but all in all, the same, dull routine. Are there days when you think to yourself, "I just don't want to do this anymore?" Are there times when you think, "There has to be something better than this?" We find ourselves yearning for fulfillment as we do not take the time to realize that we are our own fulfillment. Once you realize this, your daily routine will no longer yield a sense of feeling "stifled." Ignorance of spirit yields incompleteness.

If you feel like you've lost your ambition, remember the days when you were full of determination. If you think that your life will never change, yet you can't see yourself doing what you are doing forever, remember the dreams you had when you were a child and revive them. Take time for reflection. Recall the moments in your life that positively made you glow with happiness. Nourish your heart and mind with the intangible pieces of happiness and you will be contented.

During the humdrum day, have you ever found at times that you compare yourself to others? Did you ever sit back and look at your life to say to yourself, "Why can't I have what they have?" "I deserve better." "I should not be in this situation." Or the infamous, "I can't believe that person won the lottery! I should have won it!" Did you ever take the time to examine your life? Have you taken the time to give thanks for the things you do have? For instance, have you given thanks for that monotonous routine you are blessed to do everyday? Have you given thanks for the bed you sleep in every night? Did you remember to say "thank you" for that occasional something that brightened up your day?

It is only when you allow your mind to intercept the truth of soul that you become burdened with restlessness. The greatest love and the most treasured joys come by taking risks of heart. When you were young, you had no fear to love, that fear was learned. You looked forward to tomorrow, dreading it is what you learned to do. Greet each day through the eyes of youth. Seize every day through the vision of your spirit, not through the eyes of prediction.

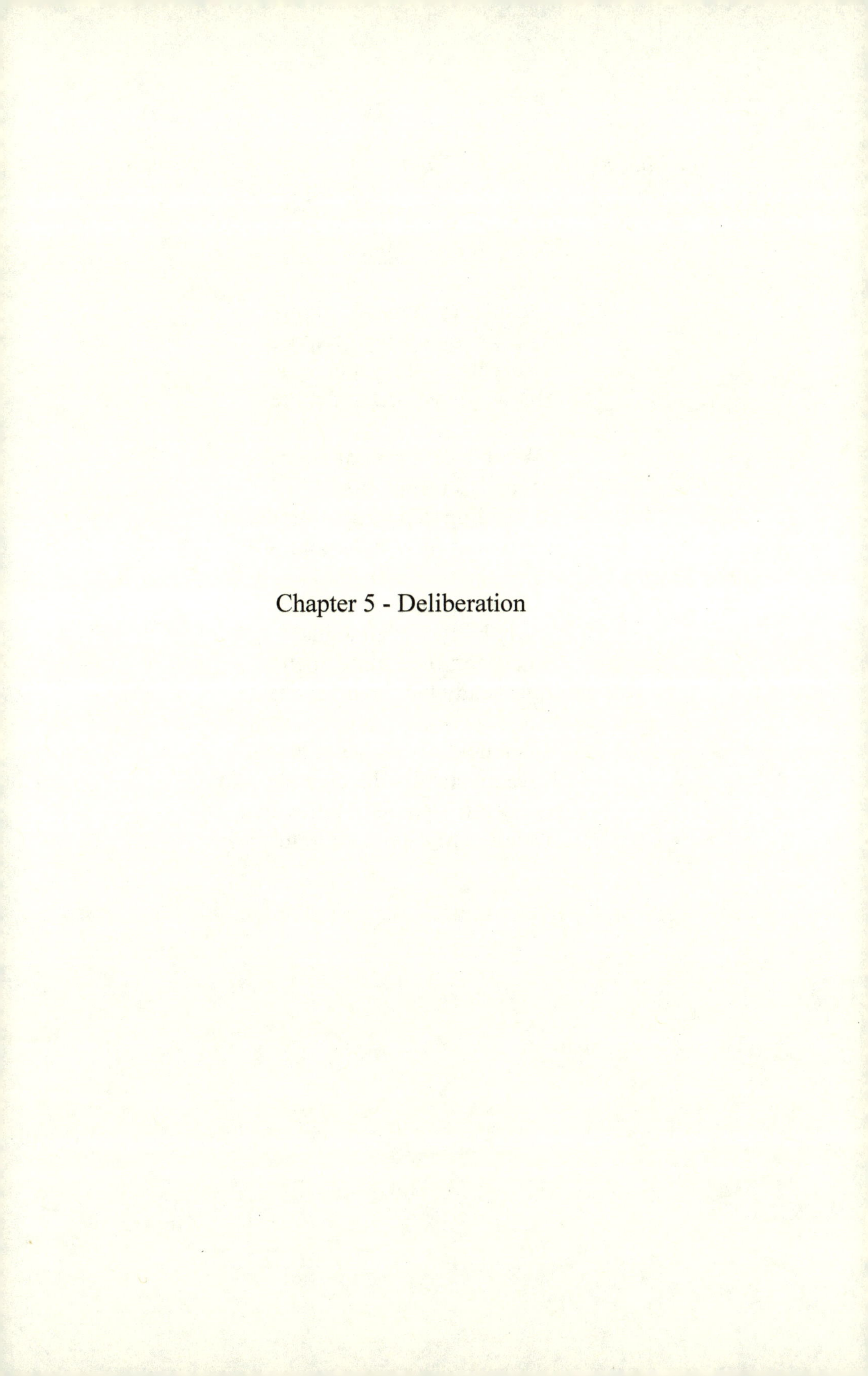

Chapter 5 - Deliberation

Voodoo

Under the farce of night,
The air so lavishly breathes -
Encrypted within moonlight,
His words voiced in tongue –

Witch's cauldron of desire,
Slowly burning his brew –
Its heeding vapors so migrate,
Into a draping cloud over me –

Sleeping doll of voodoo,
My body woven at rest –
Midnight; the tolling anchor,
While steady his flavorful chant –

When next his innocent touch,
Love mystically devours me –
Witchcraft's chain of attraction,
Devours my spirit - into his -

Ethereal Circlet

I, the nub of your creation
As you retreat into your medium –
Supple searing of intrusiveness
Smokes out the doubting burn –

Devotion or obsession, my ponder
Of your deliverance of I to me –
Daily my need begs for you;
Rendering me helpless before you –

Your native je ne sais quoi
Delicately weaves an elusive peace
Proud is your Haitian master
His most honored student –

In kneel, I fall to the ground
While mystically standing –
In trance before your eyes;
The altar of my tranquility –

My Knight: A Classic Ode

I was waiting for my knight,
You know, the one riding
The white horse –
But he took a wrong turn,
It seems in the woods and
Has been riding lost –

"Okay," I said and put my
Order in for a new one,
However, the maker replied -
That the one I ordered is
Out of stock and back orders
Are not now being accepted –

"Alright," I said and I found
Another acceptable model,
So ordered that one, I did –
Well, the maker replied –
That the one I ordered was
Discontinued for life –

"Oh, dear," I answered and
Found myself abandoned by knight,
So ordered no more, I did.

River Dance

Your shadow enflames the fire
Burning in yearn inside of me –
While I rest anesthetized
Within your magical terrain –

My awareness realigns its focus
To the majestic awe of the river –
The river aside which you danced
The river within which you circled –

Each sip of air I inhale evokes
The poison of the water you've churned –
The venom you've injected stirring
My motivation into lethargy –

You've altered me to your desire
Entrenching my focus redirected –
My mind, once a full challis
Now an array of what once was –

Your iridescent moon shall shine
Indeed it shall, despite my know –
Your doting was never enough
All or nothing, and nothing not –

Wedded

And at the Altar

Of my dreams,

I have wedded him –

My absent partner

Would You

If my name were a gift,
Then call upon same
Would you, gifting me
The pleasure of your speak
Of it –

If my heart were a blessing,
Then gently hold same
Would you, gifting me
The peace of your love,
Into it –

If my eyes were heaven,
Then tenderly kiss them
Would you, gifting me
The serenity of your soul,
Into me –

If my spirit were freedom,
Then make love to me
Would you, gifting me
The totality of you,
Within me –

If my give were a diamond,
Then cherish the same
Would you, gifting me
The know of appreciation
Of me –

If my love were your need,
Then forever embrace me
Would you, gifting me
The riches of simplicity
For I –

If my name were a gift,
Then call upon same
Would you, gifting me
Eternal happiness with you
Within me –

Just Another Day

Beyond the mayhem
Of the day –
In suddenly slips
Home's edgy choke –

Within the brouhaha
Of the dusk –
In steady silence
Rises the moon –

Usual monotony looms
Day's long end –
While Night fondles
Morning's anemic rise –

Each futile step
Withers life meaning –
Strength freely disavows
Its vigorous posture –

Within the numbness
Of the shell –
Lies a seed
Left for dead –

Vaguely Precise

I don't remember yesterday,
But I do recall tomorrow –
Holding the promise of hope,
For these comatose dreams.

I don't remember yesteryear,
But I do recall next year –
Cradling unrehearsed passion,
For life's starving need.

I don't remember today,
But I do recall next week –
Whispering the drab of now,
For only memory's sake.

I don't remember now,
But I do recall later –
When this ache so sets,
Upon finality's grave.

I don't remember at all,
But I do recall nothing –
Of how I've fostered,
Discriminating amnesia.

Quietly Numbed

The sun shines
Recklessly,
Through your eyes,
Today.

The careless rain
Frosts,
Your wordless speech,
Today.

The wistful slumber,
Befalls
Your leafless book,
Tonight.

The formidable chill,
Deepens
Its doctrinaire grip,
Ruthlessly.

Vividly Blind

These mountainous rivers
Guise their serenity
Tonight,
Skillfully parading their
Cabaret of magnetic
Ripples.

This enchanted moon
Hovers its light
Flawlessly,
While gently roving
Bed's mysteriously forming
Chasms.

The shadowed silence
Crawls feverishly about
Flavoring,
Night's melodic rhythm
Chording with serenity's
Symphony.

That iridescent star
Draws curiously closer
Listening,
To introspective hues
Bordering life's precious
Stand.

Lover

I gripped
The air,
Of my

Lover -

Ever so
Tightly,
That he

Might -

Return,
To
Breathe.

Unforgettable

The
Antique
Clock

Vividly
Reveals
Time

Without
Hands

A Rendering of Stature

Sometimes, we find ourselves measuring who we are by our standing. More often than not, we tend to place a heavy burden of stature upon where we rank within the familial ambit.

Take marriage / the committed relationship, for instance. The feelings there are either that ‘it is a blessed union’ or there is a sense of ‘incompleteness.’ Oppositely, there may be the staunch justification for staying, such as “well, at least I am not alone.” Additional feelings tend to erupt during the course of such a relationship, such as feeling restless, crowded, bored, or stifled.

Examine the single person who continually looks to find their partner in life. Too much emphasis with no gain, however, may lead one to say, “I’m done looking. I don’t need anyone,” all the while, their internal, contradictory thoughts -“There has to be someone.”

Now, let us take a look at the vulnerability aspect of a relationship. Have you ever felt defenseless to another? Did you ever feel like your partner is trying to take you over? Have you found that you allow your partner, in some way, to control you? Have you ever felt abandoned by yourself? Have you ever asked yourself, “Why do I feel this way?”

Regardless of your status, you are and continue to be your own justification for being. Internal completion of spirit yields a complimentary relationship. A uniting of self with spirit banishes insecurities not only within yourself as a single person, but also will bridge any existing gaps you feel lie between you and your partner. It is merely insecurity that prohibits true contentment.

We tend to place a high priority on our status in the world losing sight of who we are as individuals. Every one is their own reason for existing and no one other person can add or detract from that existence. Whether or not you are in a relationship does not add or subtract from the fact that you are your own reason.

Gainful relationships, first within yourself and secondly with others, are restored when you take heed of your own needs, your dreams and your true desires. You hold the brawn to restore love within loveless relationships. Taking time to devote to your spirit does not equate to selfishness. It is absolute generosity both to yourself and to all who surround you. Nurturing and understanding your core proliferates fruitful relationships. When you grow this harmonious balance, you will no longer feel internal void. By fostering a gainful self-relationship, you increase your awareness of those around you and ultimately create the contentment you have been searching for. A restless heart is healed by the reawakening of soul. Take the time to acquaint yourself with you.

Chapter 6 - The Quest

Rest Sweet, The Flail

Travels through the
Long winded air,
Dampen the cloth -
Of meaningful word.

Standing still within
Fearless sprinting steps,
Ignores the sight –
Of precious stone.

Staring silently in
Lone weeping gaze,
Hides inner beauty –
From kind's embrace.

Sharing carelessly with
Every open hand,
Leaves empty pockets –
Destitute of freedom.

Clutching helplessly onto
Breaths of fancy,
Feathers empty dreams –
When tomorrow comes.

Travels through the
Sun showered rain,
Enrich the cloth –
Of meaningful hands.

Beautiful

His mind,
Like the tip
Of a feather,
Ever so gently
Enlivens -
My skin.

His speak,
Like the croon
Of a dove,
Ever so smoothly
Captivates -
My heart.

His eyes,
Like the vision
Of an x-ray,
Ever so gracefully
Remove -
My attire.

His touch,
Like the drizzle
Of the rain,
Ever so slightly
Entices -
My want.

His moves,
Like the ecstasy
Of my dreams,
Ever so smoothly -
Satisfy -
My need.

His beauty,
Like the sky
Of my heaven,
Ever so perfectly
Captures -
My adoration.

Reflection

Calling my speak,
Through eyes of love,
Are the sounds of timidity -
Through his tearful tongue.

Begging my hand,
Through words of fear,
Is the sound of his feet -
Running hot, cold and bare.

Wrestling my mind,
Through heart of gold,
Are the sounds of awe –
Beating from his open hands.

Needing my stubbornness,
Through time of melt,
Is the sound of ponder –
Through his joyous tears.

Dimly Bright

The
Light
Of
Dawn,

Reflects
Off
Slumber
Panes,

Whispering
Hope
Within
Rays,

That
Dreams
Become
Reality.

Ageless Age

It is time that offers
Largesse to the lonely,
While it is memories
That offer loneliness.

It is fear that brings
Years of hibernation,
While it is fearlessness
That provides for dormancy.

It is hope that flowers
Today's unsettling despair,
While it is yesteryear
That continues to quail.

It is starvation that heals
The echo of lost faith,
While it is indulgence
That fails to believe.

It is time that offers
Answers to forgotten queries,
While it is memories
That never cease to question.

Though

I cannot escape
The heat,
Through the fire
In your eyes.

I cannot escape
The Dark,
Through the light
Of your lies.

I cannot escape
The silence,
Through the deaf
Of your speak.

I cannot escape
The cold,
Through the ice
Of your soul.

I can pretend,
Though -
That you truly
Exist.

Scarred

Painless,
Are the

Cuts -

Of
Jagged

Scars.

In Waking Sleep

Your ghostly presence
Illuminates my night, as
Day reappears to salute -
Its twenty-four hour stay.

Your lips move by breeze
Freezing this phantom air -
As your mind shadows the light
With its haunting thoughts.

Your murmur exacerbates
The mime of your limbs,
As fear stands still, the
Strands of my denial.

Hopeless

And so sips the moon
Of my vacant thirst;
And so sits the sun
Upon my wilted brow –

And then –

Reality teasingly rattles
These chrome plated bars;
Behind which deadened dreams
Remain wrongfully imprisoned –

And while –

Love gnaws the silence
Of its beating heart;
The chains of aloneness
Clank their iron sympathy –

And so blankets the cold
Atop my frozen enigma;
And so starves the heat
Upon my vanished brow.

Sense Beyond Sense

Following the sense
Of my blinded eyes,
I settled my sight
Upon the light of sky.

Rapt by the sense
Of my deafened ears,
I settled my hear
Within the flowing breeze.

Enamored by the sense
Of my senseless nose,
I settled my breathe
On the sun's aroma.

Hearing the choir
Of my muted voice,
I settled my sleep
Within my tranquility.

Ousted

A raspberry hat lies quiet,
Holding onto its strands-
Remembering the comforting riot,
Of last minute gripping hands.

A chocolate, tethered coat,
Adds comfort to its friend-
Weathering summer's remote,
Unwanted desperate bend.

A hush of darkness breathes
Behind the wooden door-
Where sadness seethes,
That winter finds a bore.

A Rendering of Existence

The quest for what we are supposed to be doing with our life never seems to be answered. Have you ever asked yourself these questions: "Who am I?" "Why am I here?" "What is my purpose?" "Is this all life is supposed to be?" Did you ever say to yourself, "I feel cheated?" The quest for answers to our existence will never cease and in fact, has given rise to many theories throughout the centuries. It is perhaps one of the most perplexing questions that never fail to overwhelm the mind. It is the one mystery that will never have one definitive answer for the majority, however, will originate many different answers for each individual, all being correct.

Ponders about our existence spur many other quests for the true meaning of life and most especially, seem to induce doubts about the existence of God. Have you ever found yourself saying, "Where is God when I need Him?" Have you ever said to yourself, "God does not exist?" Questioning His existence mirrors the absurdity, for instance, of doubt as to whether or not you physically exist here, for one. Do you have feelings? Do you not grieve? Do you suffer pain? Faith in your spirit is faith in God. When you ask yourself, "Where is God when I need Him," ask yourself this: "Where am I when I need me?" When you say to yourself, "God does not exist," pinch yourself and then say, "I do exist."

One thing is for certain. Each individual's purpose is neatly tucked away within the depths of their very own spirit. When you cease questioning your existence, it is then that you have achieved your purpose. If your chosen path yields feelings of timidity, fear or doubt, you need to change course.

Depression, anxiety or feelings of worthlessness abound when you do not take the time for introspection. Have you ever thought that you should be doing something else? Do you ever feel that what you are doing just doesn't feel right? That is because it isn't. To attain peace with your existence, you first need to identify your true source of contentment and then follow the guide of your heart. If you allow your mind to intercede with your heart, you will reinforce your thirst for fulfillment rather than quench your need.

Life has all of what you seek. If you do not seek, you shall never attain. Strength of purpose disintegrates fear of existence. The peace of completeness is yours when you unite your spirit with mortality. When you feel "cheated," you are not using all that has been gifted to you by the hands of God. God does not deny. When you allow your surroundings to dictate your limits, you will feel abjured. Look into yourself to answer the questions, "Who am I?" "Why am I here?" "What is my purpose?" Listening to the voice of your spirit is the key to the revelation of existence.

Chapter 7 - Fall to Rise

Reverberating Lone

Stones of selfishness
Bruised this heart,
This mind, this soul
Into a now empty shell.

Smiles seem to abound
Over this, my torment –
Relief seems to resound
Around this, my sorrow.

My desperate cries,
Dropped silently -
Though, upon
Listening ears.

Surrounded by family,
Introducing homelessness -
The occasional
Father's hello.

Softly died my angel,
The only one
To grieve,
Is I.

Left

The air grips tightly,
This frozen tongue –
As words smother
Base of throat.

The lonely tide sweeps,
This parched heart –
While selfishness killed
Two souls, one stone.

Relief spills disbelief,
Over this my sorrow –
As tears lie dormant
Misplaced in isolation.

Lacking is the will,
For tomorrow's wake –
As I stand alone amidst
Familiar crowd of unknowns.

Hollow

I followed the light
Into the distant dawn,
Today -
As Yesterday is over.

I have oddly forgotten
The reasons I cried,
Yesterday –
But, remember I did.

I vividly recall somehow
The morbidity of that,
Reality –
But, without lucidity.

I followed the moon
Into the distant sun,
Tonight –
As I closed my eyes.

Your Mistake

Those hands, they
Raised me –
After birth,
Your womb.

Those arms, they
Carried me –
Until Walk,
Even after.

Made me, pay
You did –
For mistake,
You made.

As words, they
Cut me –
The years,
Even now.

But never, pain
Like today –
When child,
You buried.

Tundra

Icicles fell, treeless sky
Spearing the tundra –
Icicles so avidly cultivated,
By frozen sun.

Rain spilled, tearless cloud
Drying the loam –
Rain so clearly marred,
By destitute air.

Moon shone, dimming night
Rutting the plain –
Moon so quietly astute,
With brazen disregard.

Snow dripped, flawless flake
Covering the tundra –
Snow so callously favorable,
Of every icicle.

True

My unspoken voice screams –
And, you hear;
My unseen tears roll –
Yet, you know.

My mind grows numb –
And, think it, you do;
My heart falls alone -
Yet, feel it, you do.

My pain grieves alone –
Yet, somehow, you know;
My soul silently dies –
Yet, somehow, you see.

My eyes see hopeless –
And, you envision;
My words speak aimless –
And, you realize.

You're there, I'm here –
Yet, my psyche, you know;
I hear your heart –
Speaking, to my soul.

Negated

My breath gave all it
Could today, as the
Reality of my insolvency –
Ran thick your veins.

My sacrament torments my
Soul now, under the
Guise of a muted voice –
In avoidance, your derision.

My heart loved all it
Will this life, as the
Reality of the hands of man –
Is my blood, turning to ice.

My passion lived all it
Could, as it realized
It could only live for itself –
The untimely cause, its demise.

My life gave all it
Could, as it has learned
The meaning of dreamlessness –
Where now it sleeps, comatose.

<u>Renovate Me</u>

Indulge my
Flesh,
So I may
Forget,
My mind –

Engorge my
Senses,
So I may
Relieve,
My heart –

Grip my
Bones,
So I may
Displace,
My pain –

Bite my
Lip,
So I may
Talk,
Not word –

Pain my
Pleasure,
So I may
Numb,
My discord -

Slap my
Face,
So I may
Not,
Run tears –

Take my
Love,
So I may
Recall,
A moment –

Imbed my
Body,
So I may
Die,
Once again.

Faith in Purpose

Loneliness must pervade the
Sanctuary of silence,
For soul must ascend
To unanimity within itself –

Darkness clears the light
With ambers of trueness,
As it is the sun, that masks
The path of absolute identity –

Pain is necessary for
Resurrection of humanity,
As it is sight that must regain
Clarity into one's imperfections –

Hopelessness is the antidote
For the poison of lost faith,
As spirit is rejuvenated
Through rebirth of heart –

Freedom is the gift of struggle
To those who beg to crawl,
For love shall make warm
That which the years have iced.

Hands of Avarice

Antediluvian brick shrouds the walls,
Carved with prophetic scripture –
Vacant are these halls where once,
Stood proud; scholars of justice.

Scholars of the divination of rectitude,
Astutely devout to altruistic sacrifice –
While gifting enrichment of soul,
By the touch of their healing hands.

Through weathered clefts can be seen,
The mystical eyes of pained disciples –
Clearly telling of the afflictions,
They bore from the hands of avarice.

Disciples of mercy as so taught,
Impaling justice with virtuousness –
Followers few of the elite, however,
Honorary, as the walls did teach.

Make no mistake, it was the hands
Of avarice holding monetary riches –
However, devoid of internal ease,
As those hands, cast their ache.

Thousands of years past, yet those
Bricks edify still, as today's few
Remain poor, bearing the afflictions,
Of the hands of avarice.

Eddy

Pilfering through lateral gray-
The strands of a cerulean sky,
Raining globules of a tender sun-
Rays hinting forgotten embrace.

Impaling artily gyratory clouds-
Jagged beads of fiery mizzle,
Decanting buried chronicles-
Atop the edge of brittleness.

Why for frailty to see way-
To robustness from under,
When even a wondrous sky-
Exists in fear to exist?

Walking aimlessly in alone-
The soul behind cerulean eyes,
Raining beats of a loving heart-
Rhythm gripping fading hope.

Pieces of You

The air you breathe
Is not yours,
But ours –
Every morsel you inhale,
Is a bit I've exhaled –

The water you drink
Is not for yours,
But for ours –
Every droplet you sip,
The same I swallow –

The sun warming you
Is not solely yours,
Thawing me in unison –
Every ray you soak,
Are rays infusing me.

The sky blanketing you
Is not utterly yours,
Covering me as well –
Every star you scan,
Are stars I explore.

The earth you travel
Is not yours,
But ours –
Every piece you touch,
Is a piece of mine.

The flesh you wear
Is not unique,
I bear same –
Every sensation you feel,
Is a sense of mine.

Discount my existence?
Forget my essence?
Ignore my presence?
Manipulate my core?
The pieces of you?

A Rendering of Pain

Just when things seem to be going alright and we become comfortable with ourselves, it is inevitable that another mountain is erected for us to climb. Have you ever said to yourself, "I'm tired, I can't do this anymore?" Did you ever think, "When is thing going to end?" Have you ever thought, "I just can't take it anymore?"

We are given decisions to make in life to test our strength and resilience in remaining faithful. God does not condemn you with pain as He also does not judge the choices you make. Remember, we are all born of free will, but are also endowed His essence. We do have the mortal ability to ignore and extinguish our light when life weights heavy. We do this when it seems that what we know we should do looks too hard to accomplish. For instance, have you ever said to yourself, "If I leave, what will I do then?" "What if this happens?" There are times when the road ahead appears too insurmountable to trudge.

Our spirit is like that of the ancient, mythological phoenix. It may burn to ashes at times, but from the ashes will born new light and vigor. There are times when we become so overburdened by the weight of the trouble facing us that we choose to trounce our spirit, essentially surrendering to numbness. Ultimately, there comes a time when we need to feel again and it is that very same spirit that reignites with newfound force.

When you wallow in the depths of life's struggles, you temporarily extinguish your chi's fire which only fuels the uncertainty and restlessness. Are there ever times when you say, "Oh, God help me?" Have you ever experienced the sensation of 'goose bumps' with a sort of chill within? That is the answer to your prayer. That chill within, those goose bumps on your skin are the fire of your spirit rekindling. When you feel that moment of peace, immediately say 'thank you' and walk your mind away from the trouble. If you dismiss those feelings, you are disallowing healing.

Focus on your internal fire to enlighten your heart into freedom. Your spirit can only become weakened if you let it and likewise, can only become stronger if you allow it to. Trust in your spirit. By denying it, you ultimately deny God and it is then that life becomes full of unanswered questions. Weakness fortifies strength for those who search within themselves.

You will never heal if you allow life's obstacles to blemish your faith. You will remain weak if you allow pain to take you over. Pain heals with faith in spirit.

Chapter 8 - Energy

Gifting Elements

Fire into rain -
Chill into warmth.

Ennui into passion –
Doubt into Faith.

Tears into mirth –
Fear into valor.

Despair into hope-
Famine into bounty.

These, my hands –
These, mine eyes.

This, my heart –
This, mine soul.

When ask you –
Of I what,

These, the gifs –
I, unto you.

Take a look –
Inside of you,

There you will –
Feel them all.

The Rose

Soothing fragrance,
Rekindles
Such sweet,
Sweet memories-

Petals so,
Velvety tenuous-
Evocative of,
Precious life-

Elfin, yet
Incisive thorns
Sited on long,
Pedestal stem-

Protective of,
Unrivaled ruby-
Vision,
Of brilliance-

Delicate layers,
Fussily unravel
From supreme
Weave of seclusion-

An inspiring
Welkin beauty-
Espy of
Flawless rapture-

An enduring savor,
Akin of essence-
Most precious–
Rose.

Doppelganger

Acute eyes,
Unraveling
The
Unknown-

Loyal heart,
Serving
Without
Ask-

Iron armor,
Protecting
Credulous
Soul-

Mystic psyche,
Intuiting
The
Unspoken-

Audible thought,
Disallowing
Useless
Silence-

Socially private,
Extroverting
Common
Speak-

Gentle valiance,
Carrying
The
Wounded-

Soothing touch,
Delivering
Indomitable
Know-

Unrepressed desire,
Breathing
Unrehearsed
Passion-

Healing love,
Comforting
Every
Need-

Open hands,
Holding
The
Sick –

Giving purity
Learning
Still
Receive.

The Audacity

Your wretched heart,
Still it beats
From the quagmire -
Your life, you defamed.

Your shamed hatred,
May for the weak
I you dare accost?
So be it, your demise.

My armor, dear woman,
My immortal hath cast
'Tis of your womb –
Not of your born.

You endeavor degeneracy,
Over this, my soul
You poor, sinister angel –
I cast thee unto God.

Invoked I did, long ago,
The Golden Sword
That which remains belted –
To right my thigh.

Your beastly shadows,
Could not pervade then
Now to never invade –
I pray your soul to rest.

Egyptian Throng

Pillars so sweet,
The Nile –
Flowing, rich
Water -

Staunch,
Worldly
Pyramids.

Green so dauntless,
The soil –
Budding, wondrous
Bloom -

Nature's
Stellar
Eloquence.

Antique subtle wisdom,
The scripts –
Legends so
Interpreted –

Fair,
At
Best.

Embellished Grapple

And I ran, and I ran –
Under iridescent leaves,
Covering my head –
Sun-soaked birch trees.

I mooched, I mooched –
For knew not where I was,
Ravens, the like –
Gesturing impatient sighs.

I groped, I groped –
Through thickened air,
Smog – voice of my breath –
My hands, silhouettes.

I feared, I feared –
Vines, life of their own,
Reaching for my legs –
Encroaching the ground.

I escaped, I escaped –
Beyond the dismal fury,
Escaping the stench –
Of pain's imagination.

This Kiss

This kiss,
Like rain
Drizzles in
The dawn -

Your touch,
Like breeze
Elegantly
Soothes -

Your arms,
Like security
Still
Yesterday's run –

This kiss,
Like sun
Rekindles,
Love's melody –

Your sighs,
Like heaven
Whisper rapture –

Your breath,
Like fire
Warms the chill –

This kiss,
Like fantasy
Drifts in immortal -

Your love,
Like an angel
Soothes
The restlessness –

Your need,
Like petals
Delicately
Unravels its dream –

This kiss,
Like rain
Drizzles in,
The dawn.

Sanctify Me

Lone waking hours spur
Surreal thoughts of you,
Fancifully permeating this -
My learned, latent mind -

Entrenching mystically my heart
Love's implicit passion,
Igniting uneven thirst –
That which begins to beg -

Explicit want intrepidly
Expands its delicate wings,
Naïve yearn basks in marvel -
An unrehearsed recollection –

Desirous need stingily unfolds
Baring traces of golden heart,
Unknown waters beckon retreat –
While ghostly voice booms evolve –

Solitary love bids redemption
Through grace of virtuous man,
Lone dreaming hours spur –
A boundless creation of you.

A Rendering of Know

When you feel that you have been wronged, do you ever catch yourself saying "that's not fair?" "Why did that happen to me?" "I didn't deserve that." Did you ever feel so caught up in tribulations that you say to yourself, "I just want to die?" Well, if you thought dying would be fair, to say that life is not fair is a complete contradiction, as our physical death sets free our spirit into eternal life. Life is continuous.

When faced with trials of the elements, it is easy to lose faith. All conditions, however, prove to be virtuous lessons for the good of our own integrity. For instance, it is fair to the starving that they remain hungry, for they need to appreciate food. It is fair for the rich to gain more money, as they continue their need to learn of poverty. It is fair that all of your friends are married and you are not, for you need to learn how to love with an open heart. It is fair that you are in what you deem to be an "unhappy" situation, for you need to learn of appreciation. Have you ever been completely broke? You need to learn to appreciate the value of a dollar. Have you already learned to appreciate the value of a dollar, yet you are still broke? You need to learn to savor every penny that makes up that dollar.

We tend to take a lot of what life presents us for granted including our tribulations. Ordeals are a gift as they teach growth. What if you did not know of pain? What if you did not know of loneliness, sadness, loss or otherwise? Think about that for a moment. Everything you have learned would not be an existence for you. All of the knowledge you have attained would then be slight, at best. Denying the fortitude buried within life's distresses denies the growth of your immortal existence. Clutching onto misfortunes, likewise, hampers your internal evolution.

Embrace your obstacles. Give thanks for the hardships. Give your heart fearlessly. Savor seclusion. Be grateful for every bit of your surroundings, even for what you deem to be nothingness. Nourish your spirit with the content of today. View every circumstance as a chance to grow, an avenue for learn and an adventure of merit. Your triumphs, your losses and your hardships are all for a reason and rest assured, you do deserve the chance to climb every mountain you face. Climb them all with pride. You will reap untold rewards.

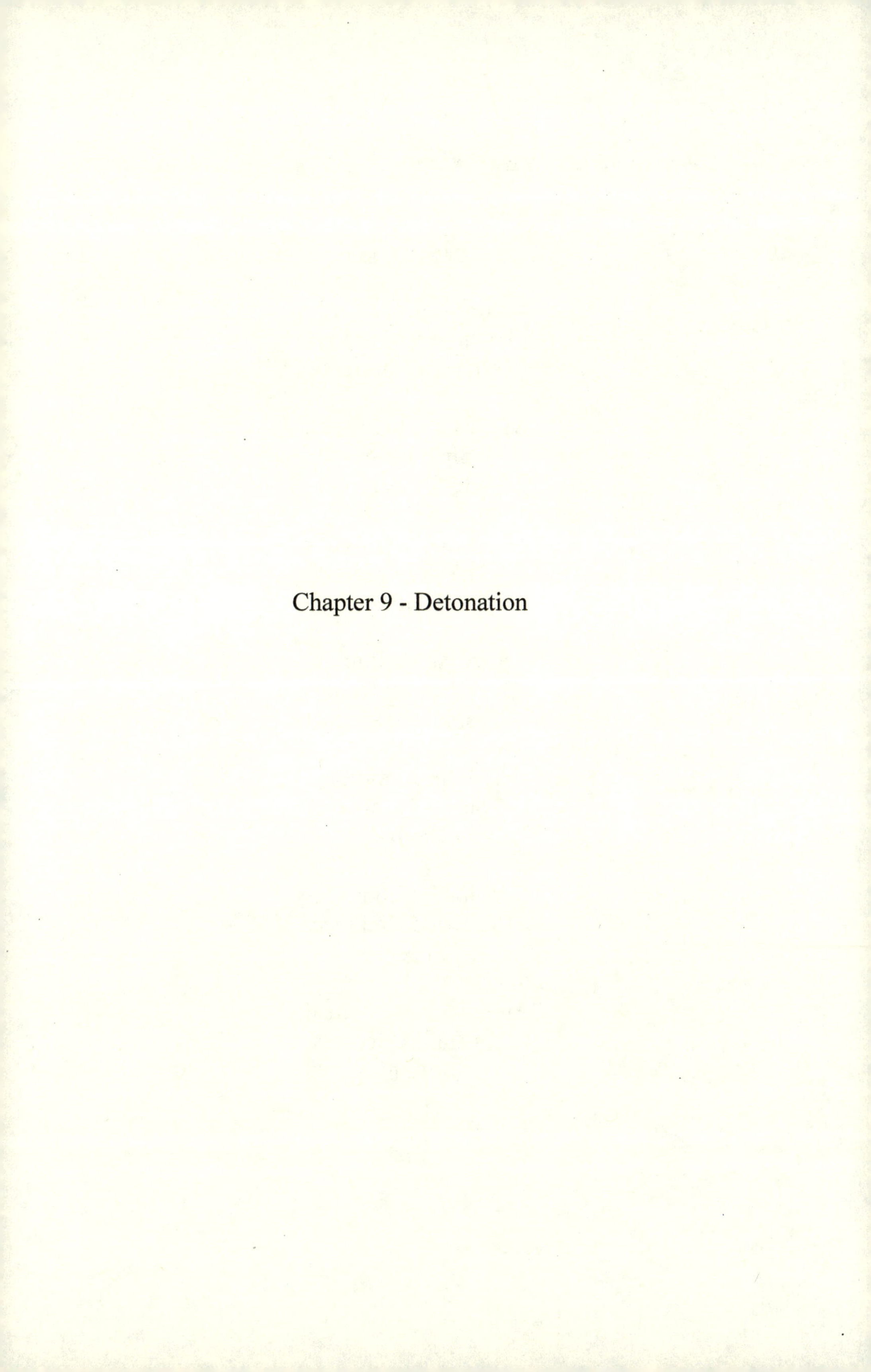

Chapter 9 - Detonation

Inheritance

Fruit is the reward
To those who starve,
To feed the hungry -

He, who is penniless,
Shall never,
Be for want -

The weak, caring for
The sick, beget
Health -

Strength shall reign
Over those enfeebled
From the taking -

The bare, clothing
The needy, obtain
Cloth -

The lonely, consoling
The abandoned, bear
Cheer -

He who feels shamed,
Yet smiles, accepts
Morality -

He, who cries,
Shall inherit,
Joyful eyes -

He, who aches,
Shall in no way,
Feel pain -

He who suffers, shall
By no means,
Weep -

Sympathy shall be
Bestowed, upon he
Who pities not himself –

Rest shall impart
Upon those of
Generous hands -

Immortality shall be
Bequeathed upon those
Who remain humble –

The faithful shall
Eternally not be
Denied -

Heaven, the reward
To the pure
Of heart.

Immortal Love

Butterfly wings, so weightless –
Free soaring into rapture,
Into magnetic embrace,
Passion so freely releases –

Angel heart, so bountiful –
Loving freely into fantasy,
Into mystical desire,
Inhibitions of no existence –

Loving sweat, so sweet –
Free falling into vacuity,
Into each other falling,
With bodies of instrument –

Butterfly wings, so pure –
Flying gently into ecstasy,
Into surreal love,
The taste of immortality.

Purged

Flanked, intrepid close –
Bemused genesis,
Fearless winds –
Pervading quietude –

False, the moss –
Weathered green,
Weeping silicon –
By hands extinct –

Careless, the ocean –
Waving dryness,
Transparent subterfuge -
Paramount obliteration -

Laughing, the mood –
Culpable ignorance,
Pontiff's vestments –
Insignia of the read –

Signal, the wherewithal –
Singed banality,
Eradicating bleakness –
Deity's conclusion.

Unwanted

Families to the right
Of me,
Couples to the left
Of me –

I walk alone.

Children to the front
Of me,
Crowds to the back
Of me -

I walk bare.

Love to the hollow
Of me,
Like to the fond
Of me -

I walk empty.

Joy to the sad
Of me,
Content to the ache
Of me -

I walk silent.

Futile is the heart
Of me,
Retired is the soul
Of me –

I walk alone.

Lay Down, My Arms

Heart,
Dripping bloodless –
Love,
Into Souls of Man –

Need,
Breathing famine -
Tears,
Into Eyes of Mine –

Feel,
Succumbing drought -
Numb,
From the lack of –

Want,
Letting go –
Yearn,
From the need for –

Heart,
Falling Lifeless –
Love,
Dies, hands of man.

Resoluteness

Pluckily ran the rain,
Upon arid ground –
Embalming authentic soul
From spurious breath -

Hollowness unable to plumb,
Life's supreme voyage -
While naïve tenderness
Saturated with serenity –

Rapaciously drank the mouth,
Of the forgotten riverbed –
Impecunious, death's lip
Many parched years –

Warriors dropped to mercy,
The feet of spatters –
Muddied hands cleansed
Iron surrendered freedom –

Enfeebled fell to knees,
Tongue to sky drank –
Tears of indebtedness
Quench drenched thirst –

The duplicitous in need,
Walking ocean's edge –
Engulfed into the abyss
God's hand of freedom.

Luminosity

Limpidness shall restrain
Tide of rancid seeds –
Pontifical sky devours
Mortal borne hatred –

Virtue gifts healing
To the emasculated -
Prophetic insight
Continues atoned wind –

Creation awes breath
A most holy mysticism –
Heaven's blessed bequest
Into hands so worthy?

Death, extended voyage
Into majestic gala –
For the unfaithful
An eternal conflict -

God, the utter impetus
Amid spirit and man –
Buoying hearts of blench
Imparted through amnesty.

Consecration

Tinctured wile in the night
Winds of beguiling rapture -
Succulent mystery lurking doom
Moistened shadows of breath –

Effusive moon deliberates
Eyes of the spectator's wonder –
Spartanly revealing quarter-loom
Precisely evading protuberance –

Quivering flesh aimlessly yearns
Demanding, thirsting, dying –
Body misted with decrepit age
A perfected vision of need -

Parched rain proving insult
Quickening winds shift –
Musing moon bitterly abides
In fullness, grants forbiddance.

As One

And if my words,
If they were water –
Would drink of them,
Your mind -

Then, what if vision,
Ours united in sight –
Would see of future,
Your eyes –

And if my hands,
If they were air –
Would dry of them,
Your tears –

Then, what if pain,
Ours drowned in love –
Thankful, would you be,
As I -

And if my heart,
If it was heaven –
Would into surrender,
Your soul –

Reckon

Spirits afire,
Celibate winds –
Coarse denial,
Hope trodden –

Spangling eyes,
Emerging dreams –
Quiescent rain,
Sun partials –

Pooling intellect,
Grappling thought –
Sneering wisdom,
Naïve conquers –

Resolve alights,
Memories echo –
Limpid need,
Love endures.

Interpretation

Pain, like a flower,
Withers to blossom –
With sun and water,
However, lives on –

Strength, like the fire,
Smokes to burn –
With wood, though,
Endures to conquer -

Tears, like the rain,
Stop to fall –
With cloud, however,
Continue to drip –

Crave, like a sword,
Dulls to sharpen –
With empty hands,
Persists to stab -

Need, like the air,
Humidifies to dry –
With arid sun, though,
Stifles the cold -

Want, like the wind,
Calms to howl -
With fierce energy,
Breathes to endure -

Calm, like the ocean,
Settles to flummox –
With stunning might,
Soothes to enlighten.

Stripped

Shower me in diamonds,
Enwrap me in pearl strands–
Drizzle rubies in between,
Do I sparkle?

Border my body in sapphire,
Sparingly sprinkle emerald-
Crown my head with gold,
Do I glisten?

Now strip me naked,
Using your bare hands-
Expose my imperfections,
Do I shine?

Fare Not, To Fare

Faring winds
Of circumstance -
Blossom unknown tales,
Of tomorrow's
Wedded lesson –

Blanching deaf -
The refutation,
Its supreme need –
Reaching forward,
Drawing back –

Living death –
Crying life,
Holding sacred fore -
Drowning on,
Fearless abeyance –

Launching aim
Desolate shock –
Typifying the immortal –
Reaching grip,
Endless vacuity –

Narcissism greets
Timorous heart –
Blossoming familiar tales,
Of yesterday's
Wedded lesson –

Shaman's Prayer

"For I am fire!"
Cried the embers of yesteryear -

Yesteryear.

"For I am energy!"
Smoked the cinders of know –

Know.

"What of I am?"
Nestled unsettling thought –

Thought.

"Of whom have I become?"
Questioned the aloof –

Aloof.

"Of where, to what I go?"
Synergy's divine intervention –

Intervention.

"Air, water, wind!"
Shouted mercy's deliverance –

Deliverance.

"For you are immortal mystic,"
Calmed the soothing angel –

Angel.

A Rendering of Beyond

You are a magnificent wonder of beauty. You are God's perfect creation. You are His pride and joy for there is no heart bigger, no love truer, of faith none stronger. You are the incarnation of flawlessness.

He has given you your road for a reason. He could have given you an easy road, but that wasn't His plan for you. His plan for you, instead, was one to test your faith, your valiance. He smiles with every step you crawl, as it will be on your knees when you reenter His Kingdom. In tears, He will take your hand and lead you to your throne. You can't very well expect to be accepted by members of a kingdom, upon a throne of such high glory, without first having traveled through the muck and mire yourself, now can you?

You need to experience pain. You need to experience being without. You need to experience poverty. You need to experience giving without receiving. You need to experience being unappreciated. You need to experience struggle and crawling; desperation; yearn, starvation. You need to experience having and then not having, fear, loneliness. At the same time, you need to experience love, faith, being appreciated, being touched, being held, holding dear precious life in your hands, being cared for. You need to experience mercy and sympathy. You need to experience being understood and wanted.

When He takes your hand, smiles at you and says to you, "Welcome home, my child," and leads you to your throne, you will be asked many questions from inquisitive spirits. How would you answer them without firsthand expertise?

Trust in your spirit for you will never be failed. Face every obstacle with gratitude. The answers lie within.

Chapter 10 – Soar

The Artisan's Blade

Blades of ice slowly
Crept in burning fire –
Under the ruse of
Chilled edges –

Swords of know tawdrily
Injected streams of poison –
Within their guise of
Shining armor –

Words of tripe funnily
Pierced through the sky –
Fogging air of truth
Within masquerade –

Water in the river
Scruffily struck the dam –
Purposely foreboding with
Drizzling disgust –

Blades of fire swiftly
Melted the artisan hand –
Under the direction of
Deity's watch –

Gallantry

The thrush sings its melody
Of an aspiring croon
To the ears of angels,
So gallantly soaring amidst –

A sovereign entity gently
Floats within the dusky
Embers, peacefully mimicking
The echo of truth –

Effortlessly flies the grounded -
Through sky of dreams
With the vision of tomorrow,
Clutching the insecurity of today –

Longingly drapes the fountain
Of a waterless hue,
Garmented with reds of know -
The thrush flies freedom.

A Rejoinder

Tinkering with shallow peace,
As night befalls the day –
Gripping is the solitude,
Within this, my doting spirit –

"I know you are tired,"
Rang His benevolent wind –
"I can see, but not touch,"
Inaudibly spoke my tongue –

"I know you are wondering,"
Sang His knowing creed –
"When Father, when?"
My exhausted words muttered -

"Less than months twelve,"
Sang promise the answer –
"Disciples," the second inclusion,
As vision of blessing remained.

Cyprian

Enwrapped within arms of Cyprian
I tread amongst the lions,
Without fear, with humbled pride,
Through the heart of Africa -

Scarce the loneliness of alone
The begging need for security,
Flailing though is the want
Though, the peace for sacrifice –

The wind excretes the heat
From my leathered skin,
As spirit continues its fire,
Embodied within loving arms –

A steady journey through desert
Uneasy path of journey,
Healing are the hands of Cyprian,
Upon my forehead, his kiss –

Abandoned

Cirrus hovers in
Distant sky –
Staunch to the
Surging winds –

Falcate the shape
To peering eyes –
Lonely is the
Coveted vision -

Sirius obtrudes in
Weathered sky –
Grayed by the
Dithering rain –

Bright the filaments
Of yearning –
Barren are the
Embracing arms –

Nascent Cereus under
Darkness cover –
Stabbing needles in
Naked brush –

Schism of formation
Derelict ruins –
By the undertow
Of hands –

Kismet

I stood to the left
Of my kismet –
Viewing the alternate
Facet of the right –

Blinded was my sight
With insatiable need -
As left's view
Ignited elapsed dreams –

My solace hadn't returned
Thought it would –
My muse slumbered
Clasping silenced breath –

Lilies budding though
In pastures of defeat –
How so the beauty
Within solitary know?

I did not trek
To the ignited right –
I held my stance
To the left of kismet –

Fallen

I fell to the side –
Of security today -
As winds dangled -
In rushing blue tide –

I cornered the bayou –
Dismayed was my poise -
As I buried my soul -
Within the trenches –

Hitherto, jaded not –
This heart of force –
Vigor sternly so plush -
Fierce the sword –

Ran sternly my mind –
Silence in the marsh –
As rain floated –
Sketchy, slothful deluge –

I timbered the sun –
With cotton grass –
Reflecting the drone –
The light of day –

Basking in the chill –
These bones of haste –
Captive, the objet d'art –
This, my solitude –

I fell to the back –
Of need today –
As winds dangled –
The rushing blue tide –

Incarnation

It escapes me now,
The call of the wild -
And does so preclude,
The distant wondering -

It hampers me, darling,
The call of the shallow -
And then you enlighten,
My distant heart –

It has created me,
My aloneness, my yearn –
And then you appear,
My forgotten need –

It ignores me, darling,
The know of my mind –
By continuing allowance,
Of my beating heart –

It escapes me now,
The feel of the wrap -
And then instinct infuses,
Ideal your quintessence –

Unguarded

It was the fever
Of the wind,
Christening my
Modest breath –

Spurring the wings
Of butterflies –
Loosely within –

It was the breeze
Of his spirit,
Caressing my
Unadorned heart –

Lulling the obstacle
Of insecurity –
Tightly within –

It was the softness
Of the ocean,
Soothing my
Parched skin –

Serenading the droll
Of protection –
My rumination –

Taut the Night

Flakes of jasmine
Pierced the sky today –
Like an icicle wind,
Frozen from capture –

Seamless rain dripped
Along the left of sun –
Making jealous the right,
Sky did scurry –

Solace ran insipid
Through eyes of hunger –
Swiftly along the rivulet,
Strands ran peace –

Settled within unease
Arid tears did plumb –
As fear ran steadily,
The mystical deliberation -

Crumbs of need
Collected the jasmine –
As winds swept clean,
Right of passage –

Resounding Blind

I love the night,
As it peers –
Through weary eyes –
Of translucent day –

I adore the sun,
As it enters –
Through leather skin –
Into drenched heart –

I sanction the rain,
For it spills –
Its misty veil –
Unto parched reality –

I serenade the wind,
While it warms –
Chilled summer air –
Easing derelict mind –

I tread the sands,
Across desert plane –
Grains of sympathy –
Exfoliate useless skin –

I evoke the snow,
Ruminating the numb –
Through weary eyes –
Tinted by life –

Repetitive Epoch

Through frost of yesterday's demise,
Clarity circles tomorrow's embrace
As today's musing continues to slumber,
Beyond the timbers of doused flame –

And yet, amusement of inveigling speak,
Continues its lifeless pour
Unto such an unsuspecting heart,
Tongue archly inhabiting innocence -

Heedlessly the night so reflects,
The braying squander of silence -
As naïve spirit carries the perfidy,
Laid upon it by callous hands –

Righteous remains yesteryear's flame,
Under the indictment of the parched –
Lowly sifting through the rubble,
Of incontestable familiarity –

The Phoenix of Raven

Scorching wind tumbles
In whirling proclamation –
Upon weathered feet,
Insidious the raven –

A fearless trace
Of sun so gestures –
Gently piercing wings,
Soothing their fear –

Like the Embers
Of a poisoned snow –
Melts within soil,
Claws they soak –

Like the ruse
Of a blossomed lily –
Prior the spring,
Shiny the black –

Like the mirage
Of a shadowed dust –
Upon weathered feet,
Ingrained the phoenix –

Emancipation

My tongue wrapped
The corners of the Islip,
While slowly falling night –
Showered redemption –

Arms of imbalance
Embraced the stifled fjord,
As animated sun cried –
Dripping still light –

My eyes heard
The scenery in silence,
While my ears saw –
The injustice –

Hands of wile
Sifted the sand bare,
As greenery turned around -
Its shamed face –

My mouth seized
Its tongue so gnarled,
While already fallen night –
Delivered release –

A Conduit for Dawn

The fields in the dawn
Brushed against the flame –
Of a distant morn,
Brooding in the brush –

Winds whirling in the moss
Reserved the boiling heat –
Of a tainted night,
Dissertating its kaleidoscope –

The moon in the sun
Palliated the deafening sweat –
Of a coarse phase,
Drifting in the shallow -

The glisten in the rain
Drenched the molten flame –
Of the distant morn,
Resurrecting light anew –

Heaven's Deliverance

"Cry once, into the darkness,"
Cried the shepherd –
"Scream twice, into the light,"
Bellowed the lamb –

Awakening

"Holler nines, the swords,"
Answered the wind –
"Sear the trepidation,"
Called the angel –

Dawning

"Hold back the gaffe,"
Whispered the prophet –
"Challenge the foe,"
Whaled the bishopric –

Rejuvenating

"Laugh once, into the darkness,"
Demanded the shepherd –
"Speak twice, into the light,"
Harped the lamb -

Reincarnation

Peripheral Edge

I fell into the sky today,
As I watched life –
Take a careless stand,
Along the edge of the river –

And I floated aimlessly,
To alongside northern star –
Whose feverish tip,
Steadily taunted my brow –

I moved along the driblets,
Of ocean's seizing rain –
Along the coast of the Nile,
Narrowly escaping the undertow –

Assiduously burned the sun,
Though, as wantonly I basked –
At the nether land nape,
Of immortal genius –

I wafted to the ground then,
Delegated next to life -
Carelessly I took its hand,
And walked, the edge of river –

Uncloaked

And as we walked
Through the cylinder sky –
There stood the silvery fox,
Cloaked in pearly white –

While we rested there
Just above gray cloud –
The glow of ice-blue,
His eyes in the distance –

Thunder, then it rang
Deafening just below us –
As fiery moon shone,
Its distant awakening –

And as we slid
Down the cylinder portal –
Our bodies, they entwined
Within his cloak -

We were placed atop
The ground so gently –
As was the silvery fox,
Without his cloak –

Contenting Breeze

It was the night,
Through crimson
Gray cloud –
That dried the air –

It was the day,
Through bright
Hazel sky –
That doused the sea –

It was the shadow,
Hovering blue
Dusk rain –
That lit the tide –

It was the wind,
Through orange
Autumn leaves –
That eased the silence –

Begging Not To Wither

'Tis a pool of disgust
Waving its shallow hand –
Within the humid plane
Of a sedentary existence –

'Tis a loveless shack
The pieces of hollow –
Ripping at the fiber
Of such bleeding heart –

A fool of a foul pride
Continuing its dance –
Through the bulk
Of wetted shards -

Silencing the roost
If only for a moment –
Where rest takes over
The harshness of alone –

Beckoning the waters
To cause a fuss –
That they may excite
This, parched heart –

A Solitary Embrace

My wrist trembles,
As my hand shakes
Distant memoirs –
Of happiness, turned
To sheer blunder –

My laugh echoes,
In chambers of tears
As here sits –
The tide of loneliness
Whilst need rumbles –

My legs hurt,
Running through my mind
Back to yesteryear –
Where love was not,
A distant want –

My heart crumbles,
As my spirit aches
For a kind embrace –
Upon this, my skin
Arid by neglect –

My arms tremble,
As my shoulders stretch
Around my torso –
Fingertips touching
Behind my back –

Tears

And I cried in the winter,
The warm breeze –
It was the wind,
The deluge of my tears -

I cried in the summer,
The chilled air –
It was the loneliness,
The salt from my eyes –

Sobbed, I did in the fall,
The falling leaves –
It was the sympathy,
For my sadness -

Then I wept in the spring,
The warm breeze –
It was my own embrace,
The fall of my rain -

Annihilation

Anchors sit, washed ashore –
As so didst the tide agitatedly –
Whilst beckoning resolve,
Within the ocher sea –

Belated cries of heed -
At the wrath of redemption –
Paramount was the oracle,
New freedom mightily augured –

Behold now, incensed waters –
Raging under pale amber sky –
Rightfully bidding the toll,
Unto the so-called doughty –

Arcane winds swept the torrent –
Endowing God's mystical rumpus –
Timely strewn anchors,
Fashioned impenetrable walls –

Feebly attempted did their will –
But were secured to their ruin –
As bleeding eyes entreated,
Tsunami tendered farewell –

A Final Rendering

There are no barriers on the road to contentment. The only obstructions are those we, ourselves, create. There are no limits as to how high we can soar. The only constraints are the ones we self-erect. Our ability to know is endless. Our power to make into reality the intangibility of fulfillment is interminable. Make today, your tomorrow.

Inspirational Quotes

Poverty in the hands
Of the Starving
Is meant for the hands
Of the wealthy
To learn of poverty,
Through giving –

* * *

It is not how many times
You've loved,
But rather,
How you've loved

* * *

If beauty were a tangibility,
Then you are
Its living replica

* * *

Strength is born of weakness
For those who search within themselves –

A life without mountains to climb
Is a life devoid of achievement -
Climb with pride and reap the rewards

* * *

Fear is the recklessness of insecurity
That binds your vision to doubt.
Banish your fear with clarity of vision

* * *

Dreams are the whispers of tomorrow's hope,
The peace for yesterday's sorrow
And the strength of purpose

* * *

When the night finds you lonely,
The sun shall rise to comfort you.
When the day finds you troubled,
The night shall embrace you.
When life finds you weary,
Love shall bridge your burdens

* * *

Intuition is the golden thread
That ignites the light of truth
Within doubt

If today should find you in need,
Look to tomorrow in hope.
If tomorrow should fail to deliver,
Remember yesterday as a triumph

* * *

Success is not measured
By the assets we collect,
But rather,
By the gifts of spirit we bestow

* * *

Your soul is flawless,
Your energy is boundless.
You are your own reason
For today and always

www.ingramcontent.com/pod-product-compliance
Lightning Source LLC
LaVergne TN
LVHW090943080826
845145LV00003B/870